Riddles to Solve While You Poop

Index

Introduction

Why not make your bathroom break a little more stimulating than usual?

All you need to do is:

- Grab this book
- Head to the bathroom
- Challenge your mind in a place where no one can disturb you!

Inside, you'll find a variety of puzzles to keep you entertained. You can choose the type based on your mood that day.

The difficulty of the puzzles is random, so you might stumble upon an easy one—or one that really tests your brainpower!

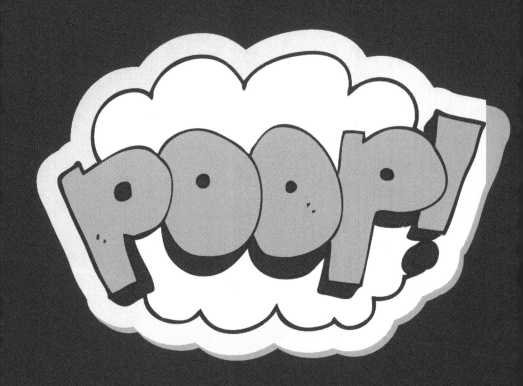

Rules

Use the table of contents to find the type of puzzle that best suits your mood. Here's a breakdown of what you'll find:

- Math Puzzles: A series of challenges where calculations are key to solving the problem.
- Logic Puzzles: These puzzles require you to think critically and pay close attention to every detail in the text!
- Funny Riddles: Perfect for when you want to engage your brain and have a good laugh!
- Famous Riddles: A collection of the most well-known riddles from around the web. These won't be easy— you'll need to pay extra attention to the details and think hard to crack them!
- Mazes: For those moments when you want a break from thinking and just enjoy some fun navigation.

When you see this symbol, it means the puzzle might be tricky. The next page will be left blank so you can write down notes or work through the solution.

Don't have a pen and you're already in the bathroom? No problem! If you spot this symbol, the puzzle can be solved using just your brain—no writing needed!

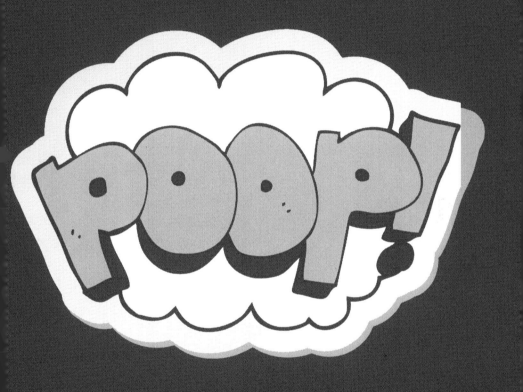

Math Puzzles

In the Math Puzzles section, you'll find a variety of challenges intricately connected to the fascinating world of mathematics. To solve these puzzles, you'll need to use your reasoning skills and perform calculations, sometimes diving into complexities that will push your mental limits.

Here are two straightforward examples to clarify the kind of puzzles you'll encounter:

Discover the elusive number hidden within the following:

- •5
- •4
- •8
- • 26

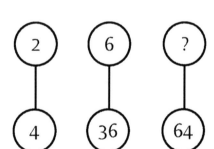

Math Puzzles

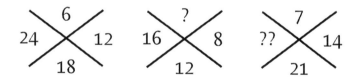

Complete the following series:

- ?=4, ??=36
- ?=4, ??=28
- ?=8, ??=28
- ?=43, ??=65

```
    6               ?               7
24 ✕ 12        16 ✕ 8        ?? ✕ 14
   18              12              21
```

Math Puzzles

1

How many squares can you find in the 3×3 grid?

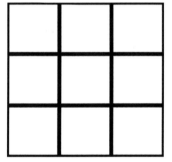

Math Puzzles

2

Discover the elusive number:

- 2
- 0
- 10
- 8
- 7

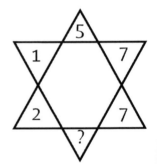

Math Puzzles

13

Discover the elusive number:

- 8
- 5
- 12
- 23
- 1

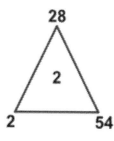
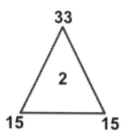
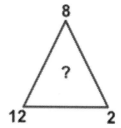

Math Puzzles

4

I have five packs of candies. Four of them weigh 40 grams each (containing 20 candies weighing 2 grams each), and one, which has been 'tampered with,' weighs 30 grams (containing 20 candies weighing 1.5 grams each). With just one weighing on a scale, I need to identify the lighter pack.

Math Puzzles

5

Julia is 20 years old. Her grandfather Enrico is 80 years old. How many years ago was Julia's grandfather six times older than her?

14

Math Puzzles

6

What is the two-digit number XY that is equal to the sum of the square of X and the cube of Y?

Math Puzzles

7

A man is walking along a road that crosses a desert. Every day he walks 5 kilometers, but each night he rests and goes back 3 kilometers. How many days will it take for the man to reach the end of the road, which is 50 kilometers away?

Math Puzzles

8

There is a family consisting of a father, a mother, and two children. The children have an age difference of 4 years, while the father is twice as old as the mother. The total sum of the ages of the four family members is 100 years. What are the ages of the father, mother, and children?

Math Puzzles

9

There are three brothers, each of whom has one sister. How many children are there in total?

Math Puzzles

10

Discover the elusive number:

- 59
- 52
- 134
- 54

	56
44	31
16	25
28	

	16
49	5
27	11
22	

	89
25	35
5	?
20	

Math Puzzles

11

Discover the elusive number:

- 18
- 8
- 16
- 15
- 12

20
12
14

12
4
10

22
?
14

Math Puzzles

12

Complete the following series:
03, 07, 08, 11, 13, 15, 18, 19, 23, ?, ??

- ?=23. ??=28
- ?=28, ??=23
- ?=25, ??=28
- ?=23, ??=18

Math Puzzles

13

Discover the elusive number:

- 8
- 9
- 10
- 4

8   4   2

?   5   2

22

Math Puzzles

14

Complete the following sequence of
numbers 6,12,15,14,28,31,30,60,63?

20

30

54

62

32

Math Puzzles

15

In a garden, there are 10 apple trees. Each tree has 20 branches, and on each branch, there are 4 apples. How many apples are there in total?

100
700
90
800
200

24

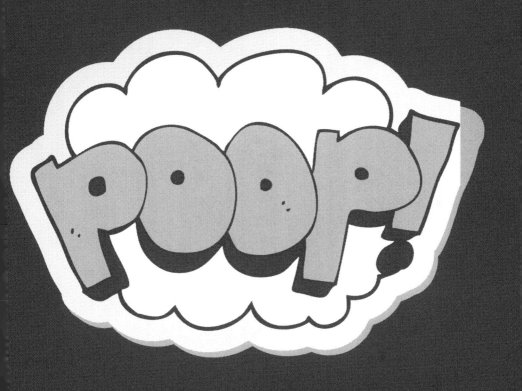

Logic Puzzles

1

Choose the figure that completes the sequence.

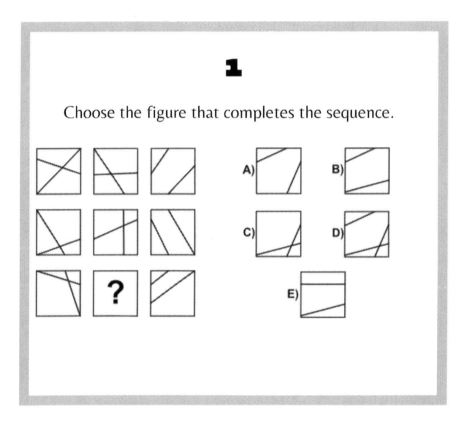

Logic Puzzles

2

Find the word that doesn't belong, after anagramming all of them

- stair =
- stream =
- stone =
- bread =
- patio =

Logic Puzzles

13

Complete the following series based on the position of letters in the alphabet: T, S, A, E, ?, D, O, I, L, ?, O

Options:
- R; H
- I; E
- V; A
- M; B
- L; N

Logic Puzzles

4

Find the corresponding value. If: CRANE = 32, then FALCON = ?

- 45
- 51
- 47
- 40
- 53

Logic Puzzles

5

Find the missing word:

- HAND
- FINGER
- EYE
- MOUTH
- NOSE

?	lip
arm	ear

Logic Puzzles

Choose the figure that completes the sequence.

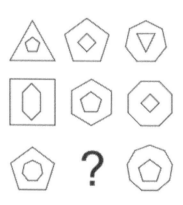

A) B) C) D)

31

Logic Puzzles

7

Let go of one of the following figures.

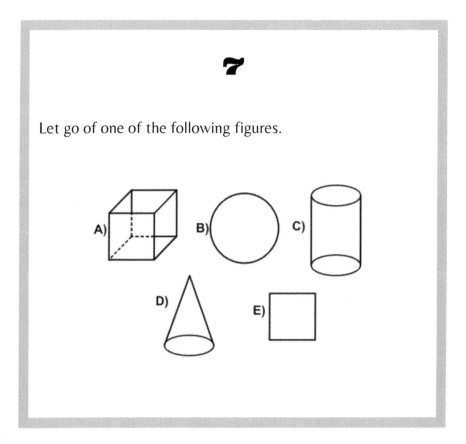

32

Logic Puzzles

8

Find the missing number if:
ISLAND = 6, VOLCANO = 12, MOUNTAIN = ?

- 15
- 6
- 10
- 17
- 14

Logic Puzzles

9

Three fathers each have two sons. They decide to go to the movies, but there are only 8 seats left in the theater. Yet, they all manage to sit down, each in a separate seat. How is this possible?

Logic Puzzles

10

On a moonless night, a man is walking along a completely dark country road. There are no streetlights or other sources of light, yet the man doesn't need a flashlight to see where he's going. How is this possible?

Logic Puzzles

11

A completely black horse jumps over a tower and lands on a small man who disappears. What scene is this?

Logic Puzzles

12

Marco was 17 years old the day before yesterday. Next year, however, he will turn 20. How is this possible?

Logic Puzzles

13

One of the following statements is true, the others are false. Which one?

1.   Only one of the statements is false.
2.   Exactly two of the statements are false.
3.   Only three of the statements are false.
4.   Exactly four of the statements are false.
5.   All five of these statements are false.

Logic Puzzles

14

Two prisoners are locked in a cell. There is an unbarred window high up in the cell. Even if they stand on the bed or on each other's shoulders, they can't reach the window to escape. So, they decide to break out. They can't dig a tunnel because it would take too long. Finally, one of the prisoners figures out how to escape. What is his plan?

Logic Puzzles

15

You have 26 white socks, 18 black socks, and 16 blue socks, all scattered on the floor, and the room is dark. How many socks do you need to pick up and take outside to be sure you have at least one matching pair in color?

Logic Puzzles

16

Molly is a mammal but not an animal, a letter but not a word, happy but not joyful, a book but not a story, coffee but not tea. So, what is Molly?

Logic Puzzles

17

Consider three boxes containing fruit. The first is labeled 'Strawberries,' the second is labeled 'Bananas,' and the third is labeled 'Strawberries and Bananas.' Each of the boxes is labeled incorrectly. How can you correctly label each box if you are only allowed to select one fruit from one of the boxes?

Logic Puzzles

18

IThe favorite foods of four children—Sofia, Elena, Manuel, and Nicol—are listed below. Each child has a different favorite food. Use the following food clues to match the children with their favorite foods.

1. Elena likes ketchup and mustard on her favorite food.
2. Nicol is allergic to cheese.
3. Manuel eats his favorite food with a bun.
4. Sometimes, to do something different, Sofia makes her favorite food with cornmeal. What is each child's favorite food? Write the name of the person next to their favorite food.

Favorite Foods:
- Chicken:
- Hot dog:
- Pizza:
- Hamburger:

43

Logic Puzzles

19

Alice is walking through the magical forest. She wants to know what day of the week it is. She stops and asks a flower and a squirrel. Now, the flower rests all day on Monday, Tuesday, and Wednesday. The squirrel is only out on Thursday, Friday, and Saturday. Alice asks the flower what day it is, and it says, 'Well, yesterday was one of my rest days.' Alice can't figure it out just from the flower's answer, so she asks the squirrel, and the squirrel says, 'Yesterday was one of my rest days too.' What day is it?

Logic Puzzles

20

The following sentence is false. The previous sentence is true. Are these sentences true or false?

Logic Puzzles

21

A sharpshooter hung up his hat and put on a blindfold. He then walked 100 meters, turned around, and while still blindfolded, shot a bullet that perfectly pierced the hat. The blindfold completely blocked the man's vision. How did he do it?

Logic Puzzles

22

Find the missing word:

- Keys
- Myth
- Bicycle
- Sea

SLOW	FAST
?	MOPED

Logic Puzzles

23

Which number completes the proportion?

Logic Puzzles

24

Select the diagram that accurately illustrates the appropriate set relationship between: vehicles, vibrant red vehicles, sleek black vehicles.

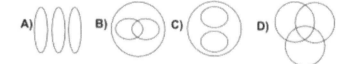

Logic Puzzles

25

Which of the following statements is logically equivalent to: 'Those who are absent are never right'?

- The present are always right;
- The present sometimes are wrong;
- Those who are wrong are always absent;
- The absent are always wrong;
- None of the above.

Logic Puzzles

26

Six books—history, philosophy, Italian, physics, mathematics, and chemistry—are arranged on a shelf.
The history and physics books are at the two ends of the shelf;
One book separates the Italian and chemistry books;
The physics and chemistry books are next to each other;
The philosophy book is next to the history book.
Which of the following sequences of three adjacent books is the correct one?

- Philosophy, Italian, Chemistry
- Italian, Mathematics, Physics
- Italian, Mathematics, Chemistry
- History, Philosophy, Mathematics"

Logic Puzzles

27

Completa la sequenza: Z, 7, U, 11, S, 15, Q, 19, ... , ...

- •O,23
- •Q,21
- •23,O
- •S,17
- •V,19

Fun Riddles

1

What has a head, a tail, but no body?

2

Why did the math book look sad?

Fun Riddles

What's a vampire's favorite fruit?

What's the best kind of music for a fish?

Fun Riddles

5

What do you call a sleeping bull?

6

Why are skeletons bad at keeping secrets?

Fun Riddles

7

What kind of shoes do ninjas wear?

8

What has four wheels and flies?

Fun Riddles

9

What do you get if you cross a snowman
and a vampire?

10

What gets wetter as it dries?

Fun Riddles

11

Why don't eggs tell jokes?

12

What has hands but can't clap?

Fun Riddles

13

Why can't your nose be 12 inches long?

14

What's orange and sounds like a parrot?

Fun Riddles

15

Why did the scarecrow win an award?

16

What do you call fake spaghetti?

Fun Riddles

17

Why did the golfer bring two pairs of pants?

18

What kind of tree fits in your hand?

Fun Riddles

19

What is fast, loud, and crunchy?

20

Why don't skeletons fight each other?

Fun Riddles

21

What do you call cheese that isn't yours?

22

Why can't you give Elsa from Frozen a balloon?

Fun Riddles

23

Why was the math teacher suspicious of the graph paper?

24

What's the best way to watch a fly-fishing tournament?

Fun Riddles

25

Why don't oysters donate to charity?

26

What do you call a bear with no teeth?

66

Fun Riddles

27

What lights up a soccer stadium?

28

Why did the bicycle fall over?

Fun Riddles

29

What did the big flower say to the little flower?

30

How does a penguin build its house?

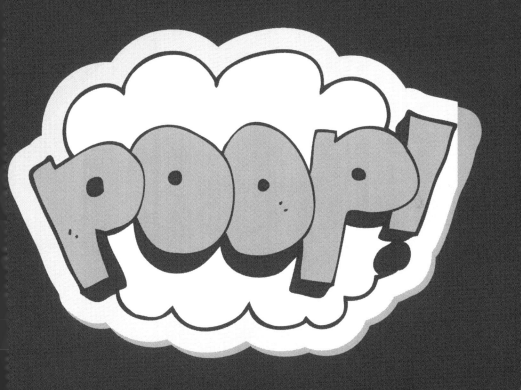

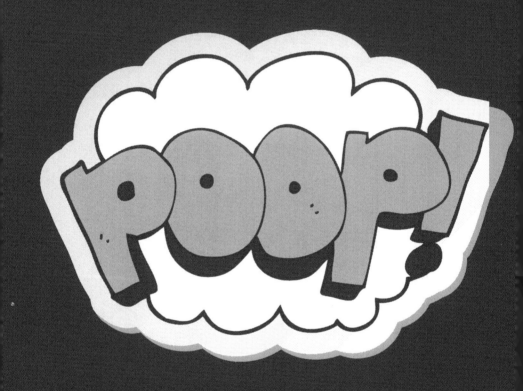

Famous Riddles

1

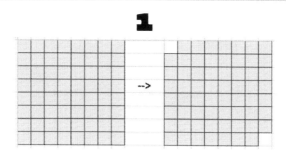

You are at your first math class at the Polytechnic University of Turin. The professor enters the classroom, and without even saying his name, he presents himself by drawing an 8×8 grid on the board, shaped like a chessboard, and then two connected squares. 'This is an 8×8 chessboard with 64 squares,' he says, pointing to the board. 'This is a domino piece, whose dimensions are exactly the same as two adjacent squares on the chessboard,' he continues, indicating the two connected squares. 'With 32 domino pieces, you can perfectly cover the chessboard by arranging them in 8 columns, each with 4 dominoes positioned vertically.' So far, it doesn't seem difficult! 'The problem is that a friend of mine cut off two opposite corners from that chessboard,' the professor exclaims, 'so the mutilated chessboard now consists of 62 squares.' The question is:

Is it possible to perfectly cover this reduced chessboard with 31 whole domino pieces, without breaking them?"

Famous Riddles

TOTO is the code that hides a natural number; STATE is the code that hides its double. (Keep in mind that each digit corresponds to the same letter, and two different digits correspond to different letters. Also, no number starts with 0).

What is, at minimum, the numerical value of STATE?

73

Famous Riddles

13

One Saturday afternoon, Lisa is on Riccardo's boat. Riccardo, an engineering professor at the Polytechnic and an old family friend, is an experienced captain. Lisa is relaxing, sunbathing, and it's fascinating to see Turin while traveling up the Po River. Lisa feels safe because of the confidence with which Riccardo handles the boat. Everything is going smoothly until, while passing under a bridge, some waves cause the boat to rock more than usual, and a life preserver resting on the edge falls into the water without either of them noticing. Exactly twenty minutes later, Riccardo realizes the life preserver is missing and immediately turns back, maintaining the same speed relative to the water. The boat reaches the life preserver one kilometer downstream from the bridge.

Can you determine the speed of the river's current without using equations?

Famous Riddles

4

You are in a dark room with a mathematical games expert who gives you this riddle: 'Right now, I'm holding a deck of 40 brand-new cards – no marks or anything that would allow you to identify them. Here they are!' says the mathematician, handing you the deck in the dark. 'Now, you need to know that 10 of the 40 cards are face up, and the other 30 are face down, and they're shuffled. You have no way of knowing which cards are face up or face down. 'Your task is to leave the room with 2 piles of cards, each with the same number of face-up cards.' 'This is a game of pure logic, so there are no word tricks or gimmicks (like turning on the light or finding a way to see the cards).'

Famous Riddles

5

An old high school friend knocks on Lisa's door. They haven't seen each other in decades. After inviting her into the living room and offering her a drink, Lisa starts chatting with her about the many things that have happened over the years. Lisa asks Martina: 'How many children do you have?' 'I have three daughters,' replies the woman. 'How old are they?' 'The product of their ages is 36, and the sum is equal to the number of your house.' Lisa thinks for a moment and then says, 'The information you gave me isn't enough.' Martina thinks for a moment and replies, 'Oh, right! The eldest has blue eyes.' 'Okay, now I know the ages of your three daughters,' Lisa says.

What are the ages of Martina's three daughters?

Famous Riddles

"You are on vacation in Africa, in a region inhabited by the Truth-Teller and Liar tribes: the members of the first tribe always tell the truth, and the members of the second tribe always lie. During a walk, you arrive at a fork in the road where a native is standing, and you need to ask which road leads to the village. You have no way of knowing if the native is a Truth-Teller or a Liar. Additionally, you remember that 'Yes' and 'No' are said as 'Ni' and 'So,' but you don't recall which corresponds to 'Yes' and which to 'No.'

What single question can you ask the native, who can only answer 'Ni' or 'So,' to find the way to the village?

Famous Riddles

7

There are 5 houses of different colors, lined up next to each other. In each house lives a person of a different nationality. Each person has a different pet, a different favorite drink, and a different preferred brand of cigarettes. No two people have the same pet, drink, or cigarette brand, and no one lives in the same house as anyone else. The clues are as follows:

- The Norwegian lives in the first house.
- The Englishman lives in the red house.
- The green house is immediately to the left of the white house.
- The Dane drinks tea.
- The person in the green house drinks coffee.
- The person who smokes Pall Mall has a bird.
- The person in the yellow house smokes Dunhill.
- The person in the middle house drinks milk.
- The Norwegian lives next to the blue house.
- The person who smokes Bluemasters drinks beer.
- The person who smokes menthol has a turtle.
- The person who lives next to the one who smokes Marlboro has a cat.

Who has a fish as a pet?
And in which house does this person live?

Famous Riddles

8

A family consisting of two adults and two children arrives at the bank of a river. They need to get to the other side and, fortunately, find a boat. However, the boat is quite small. It can carry only one adult at a time, or both children together. The children are perfectly capable of handling the boat. How can they get the whole family across the river without leaving anyone behind?

Labyrinths

Labyrinths

Labyrinths

Labyrinths

Labyrinths

Labyrinths

Labyrinths

Labyrinths

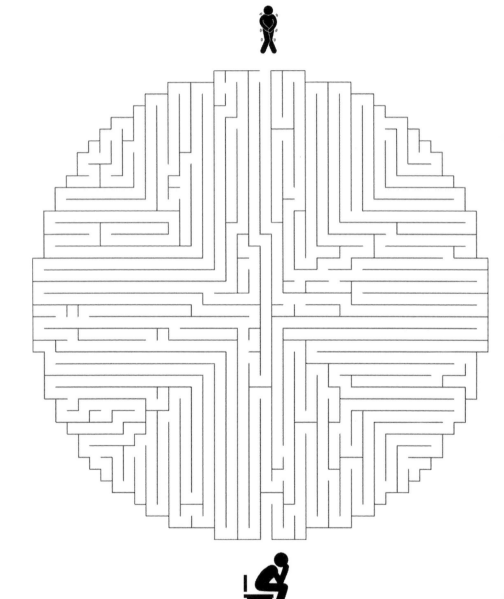

Labyrinths

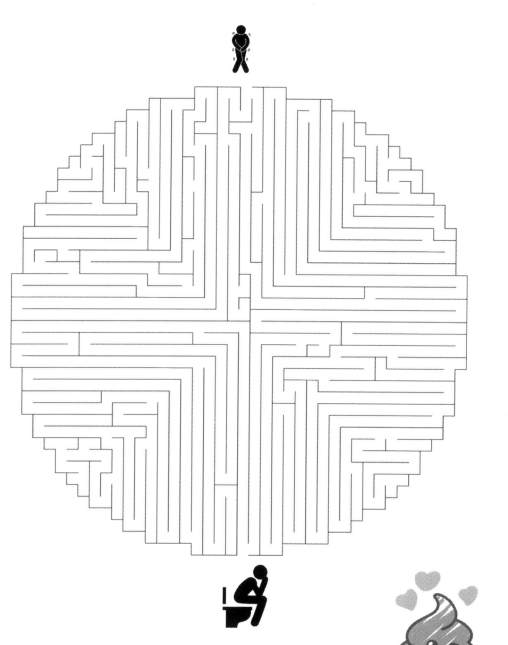

Labyrinths

Labyrinths

Solutions

Math Puzzles

To make counting easier, it's best to count the squares separately.
How many 3x3 squares do you count? 1
How many 2x2 squares do you count? 4
How many 1x1 squares do you count? 9
Now let's add them up to get the total number of squares:
1+4+9=14

2 10

3 1

Label the five packs as G, H, I, L, and M. Weigh one candy from pack G, two from pack H, three from pack I, four from pack L, and five from pack M. If all candies weigh 2 grams each, the total weight will be 30 grams (1+2+3+4+5=15 candies, which weigh 30 grams). However, if the tampered pack is G, one candy will weigh 1 grams, and the remaining 14 candies will weigh 2 grams each, bringing the total weight to 29.5 grams. If the tampered pack is H, two candies will weigh 1.5 grams each, and the remaining 13 candies will weigh 2 grams each, bringing the total weig to 29 grams, and so on. Based on the total weight, you can identify which pack has the lighter candies.

5 Eight years ago.

6 x=9 y=5

7 50 kilometers / 2 kilometers per day = 25 days.

8 The father is 44 years old, the mother is 39 years old, and the children are 6 and 2 years old.

9 There are three brothers and one sister.

10 54

11 16

12 ?=23, ??=28

13 10

14 62

15 800

Logic Puzzles

1   D

2   When you anagram all the words:
- stair   arist
- stream   master
- stone   notes
- bread   beard
- patio   patio (remains unchanged)

All of the words, except bread, can be anagrammed to form words related to buildings or structures (stairs, rivers, stones, patios). However, bread does not fit into this context, making it the word to eliminate.

3   The correct answer is V and A.

4   The correct answer is 51.

Explanation:

This puzzle is based on the sum of the positions of the letters in the English alphabet. For example, the word CRANE has the following letter positions:

C = 3

R = 18

A = 1

N = 14

E = 5

Adding them together: 3 + 18 + 1 + 14 + 5 = 32.

Now, let's calculate the word FALCON:

F = 6

A = 1

L = 12

C = 3

O = 15

N = 14

Adding them together: 6 + 1 + 12 + 3 + 15 + 14 = 51.

So, the correct value for FALCON is 51.

5   The missing word is FINGER   C   E   17

Logic Puzzles

9 One of the fathers is also a grandfather, meaning he is the father of at least one of the other fathers.

10 The man is blind! He is walking along a road he knows very well, so he doesn't need to see to know where he's going.

11 A game of chess.

12 Marco must have been born on December 31, and today in the riddle is January 1. So, 'the day before yesterday' would be December 30, when Marco was still 17. Yesterday, December 31, he turned 18. If today is January 1, it means we are in a new year, and Marco will turn 19 this year, and next year he will turn 20.

13 The only true statement can be #4. The others are false. #5 cannot be true, because it says all the statements are false.

14 Their plan is to dig a tunnel, but only enough to accumulate the dirt and pile it up under the window.

15 If the first 3 socks you pick are all different colors, the fourth one will definitely match one of the others.

16 Molly is the 'double letters' in the words.

17 First, you select a fruit from the box labeled 'Strawberries and Bananas.' If it's a strawberry, you know the box contains only strawberries. If it's a banana, you know the box contains only bananas, because each box is labeled incorrectly. From there, you can figure out the correct labels for the other two boxes, knowing that their current labels are all wrong.

18 Chicken: Nicol
Hot dog: Elena
Pizza: Sofia
Hamburger: Manuel

19 Thursday

20 Neither true nor false—it's a paradox. If the first sentence is true, then the second must be false, which makes the first false.

21 He hung the hat on the barrel of his gun.

22 Bicycle   **23** A   **24** C

25 The absent are always wrong.   **26** Italian, Mathematics, Chemistry.

27 O, 23.

Fun Riddles

1 A coin.

2 Because it had too many problems.

3 A blood orange.

4 Something catchy.

5 A bulldozer.

6 Because they have no body to hide anything.

7 Sneakers

8 A garbage truck.

9 Frostbite.

0 A towel.

11 Because they might crack up.

12 A clock.

13 Because then it would be a foot.

14 A carrot.

15 Because he was outstanding in his field.

16 An impasta.

17 In case he got a hole in one.

18 A palm tree.

19 A rocket chip.

20 They don't have the guts.

21 Nacho cheese.

22 Because she'll let it go.

23 Because it was plotting something.

24 Live stream.

25 Because they are shellfish.

26 A gummy bear.

27 A soccer match.

28 Because it was two-tired.

29 Hey, bud!

30 Igloos it together.

Famous Riddles

1 The answer to the problem is no. To prove it, we use the technique of reasoning by contradiction. Let's assume that it is possible to cover the chessboard without any overlaps, even after removing two squares from the opposite corners. Now, regardless of how a domino piece is placed and oriented (horizontally or vertically), it will always cover both a black square and a white square. In the hypothetical coverage, 62/2 = 31 domino pieces would be used, meaning there would have to be 31 black squares and 31 white squares. However, since the removed squares are both black, the remaining squares are 32 white and 30 black, creating an insurmountable contradiction.

2 It is helpful to write the multiplication by 2 (the double) as the sum of two identical numbers, aligned properly:

	T	O	T	O	+
	T	O	T	O	=
S	T	A	T	E	

The letter S can only correspond to the digit 1 (as a carry from the sum of two identical digits, which must be at least 5). By observing that the tens digit (and the thousands digit) of the two addends is equal to the tens digit (and thousands digit) of the sum, we deduce that this only happens for the digit 9 and if there is a carry from the units (and hundreds) column.

	9	O	9	O	+
	9	O	9	O	=
S	9	A	9	E	

The letter E must correspond to an even digit, while the letter A must correspond to an odd digit, different from 1.
The letter O can be assigned the digits 6, 7, or 8, resulting in the following possible solutions:

	9	6	9	6	+
	9	6	9	6	=
1	9	3	9	2	

	9	7	9	7	+
	9	7	9	7	=
1	9	5	9	4	

	9	8	9	8	+
	9	8	9	8	=
1	9	7	9	6	

Among the three possible solutions, the one with the minimum value is: 19392.

From the moment the boat passes under the bridge, it continues upstream for 20 minutes. Then, it turns around and heads back downstream at the same speed relative to the water. The return trip takes the same amount of time, 20 minutes. Therefore, the boat reaches the life preserver 40 minutes after passing the bridge. In this time, the life preserver has drifted 1 kilometer downstream. Using this information, we can deduce that the speed of the river's current is 1.5 km/h.

You simply need to take 10 random cards from the deck (of 40), forming two piles: one with 30 cards and one with 10 cards. Then, flip the pile of 10 cards, and the problem is solved! Let's say that in the pile of 10 randomly selected cards, 2 of the 10 face-up cards end up there, meaning 8 face-up cards remain in the other pile of 30 cards. By flipping the pile of 10, the 2 face-up cards will now be face down, leaving you with 8 face-up cards. Both piles will then have 8 face-up cards. Problem solved. This method works no matter how many face-up cards are in the 10-card pile—whether it's 3, 4, 5, or even none or all of them.

Martina has three children: two who are 2 years old and one who is 9 years old. Let's start by listing all combinations of three numbers whose product is 36:
- 1, 1, 36 (Sum = 38)
- 1, 2, 18 (Sum = 21)
- 1, 3, 12 (Sum = 16)
- 1, 4, 9 (Sum = 14)
- 1, 6, 6 (Sum = 13)
- 2, 2, 9 (Sum = 13)
- 2, 3, 6 (Sum = 11)
- 3, 3, 4 (Sum = 10)

Now, pay attention! Lisa knows the house number, which is the sum of the ages. Since she said the information wasn't enough, it means the house number corresponds to the only two sets with the same sum: 1, 6, 6 and 2, 2, 9. At this point, the final clue is crucial. The mention of 'the eldest has blue eyes' indicates there is only one eldest child. Therefore, the ages of Martina's children are 9, 2, and 2.

6 You can point to either of the two roads and ask the native:
'If I were to ask a member of the other tribe whether this is the road to the village, would they say Ni?'
The responses follow this logic

Strada	Indigeno	Significato di "Ni"	Tipologia di risposta	Risposta dell'indigeno	Tradotta
Giusta	Veritiero	Sì	Falsa	No	So
Giusta	Veritiero	No	Falsa	Sì	So
Giusta	Mentitore	Sì	Falsa	No	So
Giusta	Mentitore	No	Falsa	Sì	So
Sbagliata	Veritiero	Sì	Falsa	Sì	Ni
Sbagliata	Veritiero	No	Falsa	No	Ni
Sbagliata	Mentitore	Sì	Falsa	Sì	Ni
Sbagliata	Mentitore	No	Falsa	No	Ni

If the native answers 'So,' the road is correct; if they answer 'Ni,' the road is wrong, regardless of their tribe and regardless of whether 'Ni' or 'So' means 'Yes' or 'No.'

7 The person who has a fish as a pet is the one living in house number 4, which is the dark green house.

8 The solution is actually quite simple, especially if you take the time to work it out. First, the two children make the first crossing. Once they reach the other side, one child gets off while the other returns the boat to the starting point. When the child who brought the boat back reaches the starting bank, they get off and let one of the parents board. The parent makes the second crossing and joins the child on the other side. At this point, the adult gets off, and the child returns the boat to the starting side. Once back at the starting point, the child boards the boat with their sibling, and they make the third crossing together. When they arrive on the other side, one child stays with the parent, and the other returns with the boat. Back on the starting side, the child gets off, and the second parent boards the boat. The fourth crossing ends with both parents on the other side. Finally, the child who is already on the far bank takes the boat back to the starting point, picks up their sibling, and together they make the fifth and final crossing.

104

THANK YOU FOR SOLVING!

Congratulations on making it to the end of the book! Whether you breezed through the puzzles or found yourself scratching your head, we hope you had fun and maybe even learned a thing or two. Remember, solving puzzles isn't just about getting the right answer—it's about challenging your mind, thinking creatively, and enjoying the journey. Feel free to come back anytime to tackle the puzzles again or share them with friends and family. After all, the bathroom is always a great place for a little brain exercise!

Stay curious, stay sharp, and always keep solving!

Made in the USA
Columbia, SC
08 December 2024

48706818R00061